New Brunswick Lighthouses
by Harold Stiver

Copyright Statement

**New Brunswick Lighthouses
A Guide for Photographers and Explorers**

Published by Harold Stiver
Copyright 2025 Harold Stiver

License Notes
All rights reserved. No part of this book may be reproduced in any form or by any electronic or mechanical means including information storage and retrieval systems without permission in writing from the author, except by the reviewer who may quote brief passages
Version 1.0
ISBN#978-1-927835-51-7

Table of Contents

A Short History of Lighthouses   7

New Brunswick Map   9

The Lighthouses

Anderson Hollow Lighthouse	10
Bayswater Lighthouse	11
Belyea's Point Lighthouse	12
Big Shippegan Lighthouse	13
Black Point Lighthouse	14
Bliss Island Lighthouse	15
Bouctouche Bar Lighthouse	16
Caisse Point Lighthouse	17
Campbellton Range Rear Lighthouse	18
Cape Enrage Lighthouse	19
Cape Jourimain Lighthouse	20
Cape Spencer Lighthouse	21
Cape Tormentine Outer Wharf Range Lighthouse	22
Cape Tormentine Outer Wharf Range Rear Lighthouse	22
Caraquet Island Lighthouse	23
Caraquet Range Front Lighthouse	24
Caraquet Range Rear Lighthouse	24
Cherry Island Lighthouse	25
Cocagne Range Front Lighthouse	26
Courtenay Bay Breakwater Lighthouse	27
Cox Point Lighthouse	28
Dalhousie Wharf Lighthouse	29
Deer Island Point Lighthouse	30
Dixon Point Range Front Lighthouse	31
Dixon Point Range Rear Lighthouse	31
Fanjoys Point Lighthouse	32
Gagetown Lighthouse	33
Gannet Rock Lighthouse	34
Grand Dune Flats Range Front Lighthouse	35
Grande-Digue Lighthouse	36
Grant Beach Range Front Lighthouse	37
Grant Beach Range Rear Lighthouse	37
Great Duck Island Lighthouse	38
Green's Point (Letete Passage) Lighthouse	39
Grindstone Island Lighthouse	40
Hampstead Wharf Lighthouse	41
Head Harbour (East Quoddy) Lighthouse	42
Hendry Farm Lighthouse	43

Inch Arran Point Range Front Lighthouse	44
Inch Arran Point Range Rear Lighthouse	44
Leonardville Lighthouse	45
Lighthouse Point Lighthouse	46
Long Eddy Point Lighthouse	47
Long Point Lighthouse	48
Lower Musquash Island Lighthouse	49
Lower Neguac Wharf Range Rear Lighthouse	50
Machias Seal Island Lighthouse	51
McColgan Point Lighthouse	52
Miscou Island Lighthouse	53
Mulholland Point Lighthouse	54
Musquash Head Lighthouse	55
Oak Point Lighthouse	56
Oak Point Range Front Lighthouse	57
Partridge Island Lighthouse	58
Pea Point Light	59
Pecks Point Lighthouse	60
Point Escuminac Lighthouse	61
Point Lepreau Lighthouse	62
Pointe à Brideau Range Rear Lighthouse	63
Pointe à Jérôme Range Front Lighthouse	64
Pointe du Chêne Range Front Lighthouse	65
Pointe du Chêne Range Rear Lighthouse	65
Pointe Sapin Range Rear Lighthouse	66
Portage Island Range Rear Lighthouse	67
Quaco Head Lighthouse	68
Reed's Point Light	69
Renforth Lighthouse	70
Richibucto Head (Cap Lumière) Lighthouse	71
Robertson Point Lighthouse	72
Sand Point Lighthouse	73
Southwest Head Lighthouse	74
Southwest Wolf Island Lighthouse	75
St. Andrews North Point (Pendlebury) Lighthouse	76
St Martins Lighthouse	77
Swallowtail Lighthouse	78
Swift Point (Green Head) Lighthouse	79
The Cedars Lighthouse	80
Wilmot Bluff Lighthouse	81

Tours
Bay of Fundy   82
Miramichi   83
Northumberland Strait   84
St Lawrence   85
Saint John River   86

Glossary   87
Photo Credits   90
Other Books from this series   91
References   92
Index   93

A Short History of Lighthouses

There is some evidence of a lighthouse from the 5th century B.C. of Themistocles of Athens constructing a stone column with a fire on top. This was at the harbour of Piraeus, associated with Athens.

However one of most famous and spectacular early structures was the Lighthouse of Alexandria, or the Pharos of Alexandria. It was one of the Seven Wonders of the Ancient World.

The lighthouse was built in the Third Century B.C. in Alexandria, Egypt by Ptolemy II. It stood on the island of Pharos in the harbour of Alexandria and was said to be 110 metres (350 feet) high.

The lighthouse was built in three stages, a large square at the bottom, an octagonal layer in the middle, and a cylindrical tower at the top. The structure lasted until a series of earthquakes damaged it, with the 1303 Crete earthquake resulting in its destruction.

The Tower of Hercules, in northwest Spain, is modelled after the Pharos Lighthouse.

The oldest lighthouse in New Brunswick is the Head Harbor which opened in 1829 and survives to this day.

It is situated on a small, rocky island at the northern tip of Campobello Island. It was built to aid ships travelling in the Passamaquoddy Bay and It continues to be active.

New Brunswick County Map

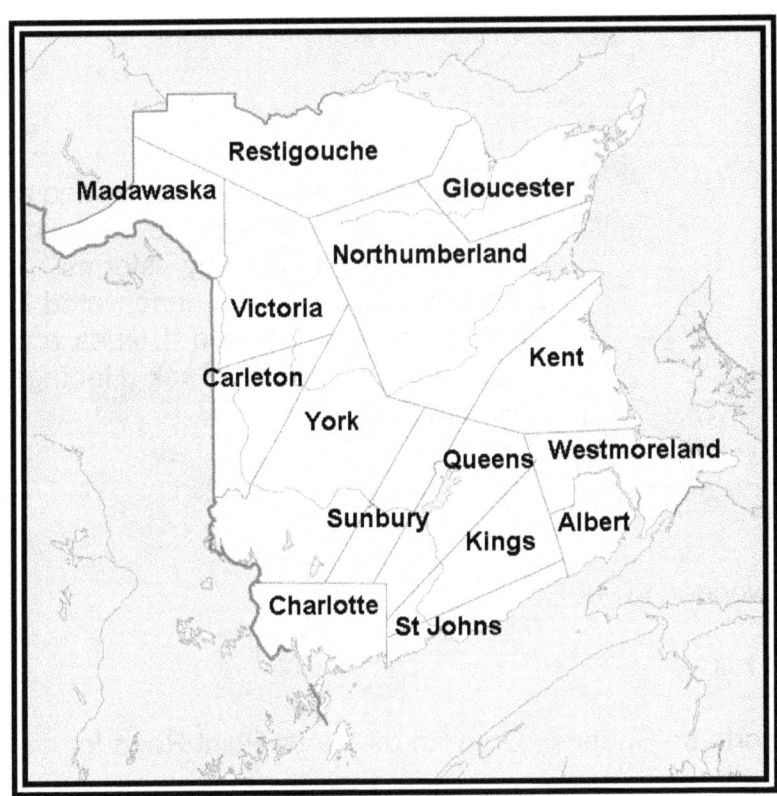

Anderson Hollow Lighthouse

This lighthouse was the third opened at it's original site in Waterside. The first two were destroyed by storms. It opened in 1903 but was deactivated in 1909. It has been moved 4 times and ended up at Harvey Bank Heritage Shipyard Park.

Description: White, square pyramidal wooden tower

Location: Shepody Dam Rd, Hopewell Hill

Directions: From Harvey Bank, head north on Shepody Dam Rd off Marys Point Road for 120 feet to find the light

Coordinates: 45°44'06.7"N 64°41'50.2"W

Opened: 1903

Automated: Not known

Deactivated: 1909

Height: 9 meters, 31 feet

Focal Height: 28 meters, 91 feet

Signal: Fixed white light

Foghorn Signal: Hand foghorn

Visitor Access: Grounds open, tower closed

Bayswater Lighthouse

Bayswater Lighthouse and nearby McColgan Point Lighthouse were both built in 1913 by B.R. Palmer of Tennant's Cove. A 5th order Fresnel lens was used at the Bayswater station. Local volunteers renovated the tower in 2011 and 2019. The station has a historical designation.

Description: White square tower

Location: Just south of Bayswater

Directions: From Bayswater, head south on NB-845 E for 400 meters to the lighthouse

Coordinates: 45°21'02.0"N 66°08'01.0"W

Opened: 1913

Automated: c.1924

Deactivated: 2005

Height: 8 meters, 25 feet

Focal Height: 11 meters, 35 feet

Signal: Red flash

Foghorn Signal: N/A

Visitor Access: Grounds open, tower closed

Belyea's Point Lighthouse

Belyeas Point is located at the southern end of Long Reach on the Saint John River that runs along the west side of the Kingston Peninsula. The lighthouse was built to aid ships in passing Purdy's Shoal on the other side of the river. The first two towers at this site were destroyed by flooding and the present tower was built at a higher elevation.

Description: White square tower

Location: Saint John River

Directions: From Morrisdale, head SW on NB-102 S for 180 meters and turn left onto Morrisdale Beach Rd. After 120 meters turn right onto Lighthouse Ln to find the site

Coordinates: 45°22'41.0"N 66°12'58.0"W

Opened: 1930s

Automated: 1930s

Deactivated: Active

Height: 12 meters, 39 feet

Focal Height: 13 meters, 43 feet

Signal: Green flash every 5 seconds (Operates at night only)

Foghorn Signal: N/A

Visitor Access: Grounds open, tower closed

Big Shippegan Lighthouse

The original lighthouse was opened in 1872 to aid ships entering the south entrance to Shippegan Harbor. In 1905 a new taller replacement tower was built by Honore Duguay. It was equipped with a third-order Fresnel lens. A new keeper's dwelling was erected at the station in 1924 by P.G. Robichaud. The site has been recognized as a federal heritage building of Canada.

Description: White octagonal tower

Location: Lamèque Island

Directions: From Chiasson, head SW on Chem. Chiasson for 1.6 km and turn left onto Domitien Ln where the light is 850 meters

Coordinates: 47°43'20.0"N 64°39'38.0"W

Opened: 1905 (Original 1872)

Automated: c.1937

Deactivated: Active

Height: 16 meters, 52 feet

Focal Height: 16 meters, 52 feet

Signal: White flash every 5 seconds

Foghorn Signal: N/A

Visitor Access: Grounds open, tower closed

Black Point Lighthouse

Black Point Light is situated at the northern end of Lamèque Island where it aids ships travelling to the western entrance to Miscou Harbour. The original Lighthouse was opened in 1872 but was replaced by a skeleton tower in 1967.

Description: Skeleton Tower

Location: Lamèque Island

Directions: From Petite-Rivière-de-l'Ile, head east on NB-313 N for 1.9 km and turn left onto Chem. Light and the light is 300 meters

Coordinates: 47°53'07.0"N 64°37'24.0"W

Opened: 1967 (Original 1872 seen above)

Automated: 1967

Deactivated: Active

Height: 16 meters, 54 feet

Focal Height: 17.7 meters, 58 feet

Signal: White flash every 6 seconds

Foghorn signal: N/A

Visitor Access: Grounds open, tower closed

Bliss Island Lighthouse

Head Harbour Lighthouse was built on the northern tip of Campobello Island in 1828 to mark the southern side of the northern entrance to Passamaquoddy Bay. The original Bliss Island Lighthouse was constructed in 1871 to mark the northern side of this entrance. In 1872, a signal gun was added for fog warning. The present Bliss Island Lighthouse, a square tower built into the concrete fog alarm building, was built in 1964 and is still active.

Description: Square skeleton tower

Location: Bliss Island

Directions: Accessible by boat

Coordinates: 45°01'07.0"N 66°51'01.0"W

Opened: 1964 (Original 1871)

Automated: 1964

Deactivated: Active

Height: 16 meters, 54 feet

Focal Height: 18 meters, 58 feet

Signal: Red flash every four seconds (Night only, year around)

Foghorn Signal: Discontinued

Visitor Access: Grounds open, tower closed

Bouctouche Bar Lighthouse

Bouctouche Bar is a 7 mile sandbar connected to the mainland. In 1902 the Bouctouche Bar Lighthouse was established at the southern tip to aid ships entering the safe harbour of Bouctouche Bar.

Description: White, square pyramidal tower

Location: Bouctouche Bar

Directions: Accessible by boat

Coordinates: 46°27'40.0"N 64°36'46.0"W

Opened: 1902

Automated: 1957

Deactivated: 2020

Height: 11 meters, 36 feet

Focal Height: 12 meters, 38 feet

Signal: White flash every 4 seconds

Foghorn signal: N/A

Visitor Access: Grounds open, tower closed

Caisse Point Lighthouse

Caisse Point Lighthouse was established in 1872 to guide ships to the entrance to Shediac Bay. The first keeper, Charles P. LeBlanc, served for 38 years. A manual foghorn was added to the site in 1900. It is on private property but can be easily photographed from the road.

Description: White, square pyramidal tower

Location: Caisse Point

Directions: From Bourgeois, head NW on NB-530 N for 700 m and turn right onto Chem. de la Côte. In 240 meters, turn right onto Light House Dr and the Light.

Coordinates: 46°19'11.4"N 64°30'45.5"W

Opened: 1872

Automated: 1936

Deactivated: Active

Height: 12 meters, 39 feet

Focal Height: 14 meters, 47 feet

Signal: 2 yellow flashes every 12 seconds

Foghorn signal: Manual foghorn

Visitor Access: Grounds open, tower closed

Campbellton Range Rear Lighthouse

The first set of Campbellton Range Lights were built in 1879 by Peter Naduux. In 1895, the rear range tower was moved from Moffat's Wharf to Kilgour Shive's wharf and in 1900 the tower was raised 15 feet. In 1985 the City of Campbeltton turned the dwelling into a youth hostel. Due to high operating costs, the hostel was closed in 2016.

Description: White tower

Location: Campbellton

Directions: 1 Ritchie Street, Campbellton

Coordinates: 48°00'36.0"N 66°40'19.0"W

Opened: 1985 (Original 1879)

Automated: 1924

Deactivated: 2013

Height: 15 meters, 50 feet

Focal Height: 18 meters, 58 feet

Signal: Fixed yellow

Foghorn Signal: N/A

Visitor Access: Grounds open, tower closed

Cape Enrage Lighthouse

Requests from ship owners for a lighthouse at Cape Enrage were made as Cape Enrage extended at least a third of the way across Chignecto Bay and was a dangerous hazard. The Cape Enrage Lighthouse was opened in 1840. In 1870 the original was replaced and equipped with a 4th order Fresnel Lens. A fog alarm was added in 1874 and it was upgraded in 1988. An adventure program including climbing and rappelling was introduced in the 1990s. The light is still active.

Description: White square tower

Location: Cape Enrage

Directions: From Cape Enrage, head southeast on Cape Enrage Rd for 4.7 km and the site

Coordinates: 45°35'38.0"N 64°46'48.0"W

Opened: 1868

Automated: 1988

Deactivated: Active

Height: 9 meters, 30 feet

Focal Height: 49 meters, 161 feet

Signal: Green flash every 6 seconds

Foghorn Signal: 3 blasts every 60 seconds

Visitor Access: Grounds and tower open

Cape Jourimain Lighthouse

In 1965, John Page, Chief Engineer of Public Works recommended that a lighthouse be built at Cape Jourimain as the area had dangerous sandbars. In 1870 the Cape Jourimain Lighthouse was first lit. On June 14, 1875, Keeper John Bent and three others drowned while returning to the lighthouse. In 1876 a new larger lantern room was built and the lighting was upgraded. Extensive work was done to rehabilitate the site in 1895 and the lighting equipment was again upgraded.

Description: White, octagonal wooden tower

Location: Bayfield

Directions: From Bayfield, head west on NB-955 for 1.6 km and turn right onto the Trans-Canada Highway. After 3.3 km take exit 51 to find the bridge

Coordinates: 46°09'27.0"N 63°48'24.0"W

Opened: 1878

Automated: 1970

Deactivated: 1997

Height: 16 meters, 53 feet

Focal Height: 21 meters, 68 feet

Signal: White flash every 6 seconds

Foghorn signal: N/A

Visitor Access: Grounds open, tower open seasonably

Cape Spencer Lighthouse

The current Cape Spencer Lighthouse, built in 1983, is the 3rd tower at this site. The 1st was opened in 1873 and the 2nd in 1918. A fog alarm building was added to the site in 1916. It was destroyed by fire in 1927 but replaced the next year. The lighthouse is still active.

Description: Red and white cylindrical tower

Location: Cape Spencer

Directions: From Cape Spencer, head south on Red Head Rd for 350 meters to find the site

Coordinates: 45°11'42.9"N 65°54'35.5"W

Opened: 1983

Automated: 1983

Deactivated: Active

Height: 12 meters, 39 feet

Focal Height: 62 meters, 203 feet

Signal: White flash every 11 seconds

Foghorn Signal: 3 two second blasts every 60 seconds

Visitor Access: Grounds open, tower closed

Cape Tormentine Range Lights

Rear Range

Both the front and back towers at Cape Tormentine were opened in 1919 after ferry terminals were established between New Brunswick and Prince Edward Island. The present front light, a short pepper-pot style tower, was put in place in the 1940s. Both lights were deactivated in 1997 after the Confederation Bridge opened. After local requests the front was reactivated in 1998

Rear Range

Front Range

Description: Square tower

Description: Quadrangular tower

Location: Cape Tormentine

Location: Cape Tormentine

Directions: From Cape Tormentine, head NW on Old Ferry Rd for 300 meters for the Outer Light. Continue for 1 km to the Inner Light

Coordinates: 46°08'06.0"N 63°46'20.0"W

Coordinates: 46°07'53.3"N 63°47'06.4"W

Opened: 1940s

Opened: 1919

Automated: ca1959

Automated: ca1959

Deactivated: 1997

Deactivated: 1997 Reactivated 1998

Height: 10 meters, 32 feet

Height: 11 meters, 36 feet

Focal Height: Not known

Focal Height: 12 meters, 39 feet

Signal: Fixed white

Signal: Red flash every 2 seconds

Visitor Access: Grounds open, tower closed

Visitor Access: Grounds open, tower closed

Caraquet Island Lighthouse

The original Caraquet Island Lighthouse was built in 1870 by Daly and Carter and was erected to aid ships approaching Caraquet Harbour. The tower was 43 feet high. This lighthouse was replaced by the present skeletal tower in the 1950s.

Description: Skeleton tower

Location: Caraquet Island

Directions: Accessible by boat

Coordinates: 47°49'22.0"N 64°54'16.0"W

Opened: 1950s

Automated: 1950s

Deactivated: Active

Height: 14 meters, 47 feet

Focal Height: 15 meters, 48 feet

Signal: Fixed white

Foghorn Signal: N/A

Visitor Access: Grounds open, tower closed

Caraquet Range Lights

J. R. Chiasson was given a contract in 1902 for the construction of range lights to lead into the harbour at Lower Caraquet by way of Caraquet Channel. John Kelly, Inspector of Lights, ended up doing the work after Chiasson was unable to. The lights opened on September 24, 1903. The Rear Range Light was replaced by skeleton tower in 2000 and the old tower was given to the town of Bas-Caraquet, where it was moved to a park

Front Range

Description: Square wooden tower

Location: Bas-Caraquet

Rear Range

Description: Square wooden tower

Location: Bas-Caraquet

Directions: For Front Range, head north on All. Maxime from NB-145 for 750 m. and for Rear Range head north on Rue Lanteigne for 350 m.

Coordinates: 47°48'29.8"N 64°50'27.9"W

Opened: 1903

Automated: 1923

Deactivated: Active

Height: 8 meters, 27 feet

Focal Height: 8 meters, 27 feet

Signal: Fixed yellow

Foghorn Signal: N/A

Visitor Access: Grounds open, tower closed

Coordinates: 47°48'16.0"N 64°49'29.0"W

Opened: 1903

Automated: 1923

Deactivated: 2000

Height: 14 meters, 45 feet

Focal Height: 21 meters, 70 feet

Signal: Fixed yellow

Foghorn Signal: N/A

Visitor Access: Grounds open, tower closed

Cherry Island Lighthouse

The Cherry Island Lighthouse began life as a fog tower in 1903. It was built to aid ships in entering the St. Croix River. A light was added to the tower in 1969.

Description: White cylindrical tower

Location: Cherry Island

Directions: Accessible by boat

Coordinates: 44°55'07.2"N 66°58'00.0"W

Opened: Light added to fog tower in 1969

Automated: 1969

Deactivated: Active

Height: 5 meters, 17 feet

Focal Height: Not known

Signal: White flash every 5 seconds

Foghorn Signal: 2 second blast every 18 seconds

Visitor Access: Closed

Cocagne Range Front Lighthouse

The Department of Marine and Fisheries decided to put range lights at Cocagne for ships using the Cocagne Harbour. These opened in 1907 with the Front Range equipped with a 6th order lens showing a fixed yellow signal. The lights were discontinued in 2018 and in 2019 the Front Range tower was moved to its present location.

Description: Square wooden tower

Location: Cocagne

Directions: From Côte-d'Or, head south on NB-535 S for 1.7 km and turn left onto Ch Arena and the site

Coordinates: 46°20'01.1"N 64°37'32.4"W

Opened: 1907

Automated: 1963

Deactivated: Active

Height: 7 meters, 23 feet

Focal Height: 8 meters, 26 feet

Signal: Fixed yellow

Foghorn signal: N/A

Visitor Access: Grounds open, tower closed

Courtenay Bay Breakwater Lighthouse

The tower at the tip of the Courtenay Bay Breakwater was built to look like a lighthouse but functioned as a battery against enemy attacks. A red flashing light is shone from the tower at present. There is no public access but the lighthouse can be seen from the water or more distant views from the Saint John waterfront.

Description: White hexagonal tower

Location: Saint John

Directions: Accessible by boat

Coordinates: 45°15'26.0"N 66°02'42.0"W

Opened: 1927

Automated: 1927

Deactivated: Active

Height: 10 meters, 32 feet

Focal Height: 13 meters, 43 feet

Signal: Red flash every 4 seconds

Foghorn Signal: N/A

Visitor Access: Closed

Cox Point Lighthouse

In 1871 a Lighthouse was built at Cox Point at Grand Lake as part of a group of minor lights providing aid to navigation along the Saint John River. In 1917 the tower was replaced by a concrete tower showing a fixed white light which was subsequently changed to a red flash every 4 seconds. It is still active.

Description: Triangular skeleton tower

Location: Cumberland Bay

Directions: From Cumberland Bay, head NW on NB-10 W for 600 m and turn left onto Cox Point Rd where the light is 10.5 km.

Coordinates: 46°01'02.6"N 65°59'43.8"W

Opened: 1917

Automated: 1917

Deactivated: Active

Height: 3.5 meters, 11.5 feet

Focal Height: 9.4 meters, 31 feet

Signal: Red flash every 4 seconds

Foghorn signal: N/A

Visitor Access: Grounds open, tower closed

Dalhousie Wharf Lighthouse

In 1879 6 towers were budgeted to aid traffic on the Restigouche River, including 2 range lights at Dalhousie. In 1909, Patrick B. Troy erected a 23 foot wooden lighthouse tower on the Government Wharf and the two range lights were deactivated. The lighthouse was decommissioned in 1960 and John Audet purchased it and moved it to his property.

Description: White, square wooden tower

Location: Baie des Chaleurs

Directions: From Upper Charlo, head SW on Chaleur St/NB-134 S for 500 m. and turn on unnamed road and see the lighthouse

Coordinates: 48°00'13.0"N 66°20'21.0"W

Opened: 1909

Automated: 1938

Deactivated: 1960

Height: 11 meters, 35 feet

Focal Height: 10 meters, 34 feet

Signal: 2 flashes every 30 seconds

Foghorn signal: N/A

Visitor Access: Closed

Deer Island Point Lighthouse

Deer Island Point Light is a minor light found at the Southern point of Deer Island, Passamaquoddy Bay. It continues to be active.

Description: White cylindrical tower

Location: Deer Island

Directions: Accessible by boat

Coordinates: 44°55'31.4"N 66°59'05.4"W

Opened: 2019

Automated: 2019

Deactivated: Active

Height: 6 meters, 20 feet

Focal Height: 9 meters, 31 feet

Signal: Red flash every 12 seconds

Foghorn signal: N/A

Visitor Access: Grounds open, tower closed

Dixon Point Range Lights

The Dixon Point Range Lights were established to guide ships to the entrance of Buctouche Harbour. The rear range tower was deactivated and sold for $1 into private hands and the owners have restored it. The Front Range is still active.

Rear Range

Front Range

Description: White, square pyramidal tower

Location: Dixon Point

Directions: From Dixon Point, head northeast on NB-535 S and the site is 1.9 km

Coordinates: 46°27'24.0"N 64°39'03.0"W

Opened: 1919

Automated: 1962

Deactivated: Active

Height: 10 meters, 33 feet

Focal Height: 11 meters, 36 feet

Signal: White flash every 5 seconds

Foghorn Signal: N/A

Visitor Access: Closed

Rear Range

Description: White, square pyramidal tower

Location: Dixon Point

Coordinates: 46°27'24.0"N 64°39'03.0"W

Opened: 1919

Automated: 1962

Deactivated: Active

Height: 9 meters, 30 feet

Focal Height: 10 meters, 33 feet

Signal: N/A

Foghorn Signal: N/A

Visitor Access: Closed

Fanjoys Point Light

In 1873 a wooden tower was opened at Fanjoys Point on Grand Lake as part of a system of lights between Saint John and Fredericton. The original tower at Fanjoys Point was replaced with an automated tower in 1971.

Description: Cylindrical tower, red and white horizontal bands

Location: Waterborough

Directions: From Waterborough, head SW on Rte 105 N/NB-105 N for 550 meters and turn right onto Fanjoys Point Rd where the site is 750 meters

Coordinates: 45°54'28.1"N 66°01'22.1"W

Opened: 1971

Automated: 1971

Deactivated: Active

Height: 7 meters, 24 feet

Focal Height: 12 meters, 40 feet

Signal: 2 second red flash every 4 seconds

Foghorn signal: N/A

Visitor Access: Grounds open, tower closed

Gagetown Lighthouse

In the late 1800s and early 1900s, Gagetown was a steamboat stop between Fredericton and Saint John. In 1895 the first Gagetown Lighthouse was built to aid ships making a large turn at this point. A flood washed away the lighthouse but it was put back in place in the same year. In 1934 the tower was destroyed by ice and was replaced by the current automated tower which remains active.

Description: White square tower

Location: Gagetown

Directions: From Gagetown, head south on NB-102 S for 1.3 km and turn left onto Ferry Rd were the site is 600 meters

Coordinates: 45°46'07.0"N 66°08'25.0"W

Opened: 1934

Automated: 1934

Deactivated: Active

Height: 9.7 meters, 32 feet

Focal Height: 12 meters, 39 feet

Signal: Fixed green

Foghorn signal: N/A

Visitor Access: Grounds open, tower closed

Gannet Rock Lighthouse

There are a large number of hazards at the western entrance to the Bay of Fundy and in 1831 the Gannet Rock Lighthouse was erected to aid ships in this area. In 1845 a 12 foot granite wall was built around the tower to secure it from the dangerous gales in winter. It was automated in 1996 and remains active

Description: Octagonal tower

Location: Gannet Rock

Directions: Accessible by boat

Coordinates: 44°30'37.0"N 66°46'54.0"W

Opened: 1831

Automated: 1996

Deactivated: Active

Height: 23 meters, 75 feet

Focal Height: 28 meters, 93 feet

Signal: Red flash every 4 seconds

Foghorn Signal: 3 blasts every 60 seconds

Visitor Access: Closed

Grand Dune Flats Range Front Light

Ships travelling through Miramichi Bay to the Miramichi River pass through hazardous Grand Dune Flats. In 1884 a channel was dredged at Grand Dune Flats. The Grand Dune Flats Range Front Light was built by A. Fitzgerald to mark the channel in 1916. When the lighthouse was deactivated, it was sold to private ownership and eventually moved to the present location.

Description: White, square wooden dwelling

Location: Burnt Church

Directions: From Burnt Church, head SW on Church River Rd for 550 meters and turn left onto Bayview Dr to find the site

Coordinates: 47°11'41.0"N 65°08'07.0"W

Opened: 1916

Automated: 1956

Deactivated: 1950s

Height: 12 meters, 38 feet

Focal Height: 11 meters, 35 feet

Signal: Red flash every 4 seconds

Foghorn Signal: N/A

Visitor Access: Closed (Viewable from public road)

Grande-Digue Lighthouse

The Grande-Digue Lighthouse is not a thing of beauty but it is the last surviving example of a type of light which used to be common in New Brunswick. In 2007 it was donated to Le Musée des Pionniers, where it was restored and placed on permanent exhibit

Description: Square wooden building

Location: Grande-Digue

Directions: From Grande-Digue, head south on NB-530 S for 0.5 km and the site

Coordinates: 46°17'41.0"N 64°33'38.0"W

Opened: 1912

Automated: 1912

Deactivated: 1950s

Height: 6 meters, 20 feet

Focal Height: Not known

Signal: Fixed

Foghorn signal: N/A

Visitor Access: Open

Green's Point (Letete Passage) Lighthouse

Letete Passage is a passage used by vessels to enter Passamaquoddy Bay and in 1879 D. W. Clark constructed a fog alarm building which blasted a signal every 30 seconds in fog. In 1903 C. L McKeen built the current wooden octagonal tower. After the station was deactivated in 1996, it was used for the Marine and Coastal Interpretive Center

Description: White tower

Location: Letete Passage

Directions: From the Deer Island Ferry Terminal, head east on NB-172 N for 350 meters and turn right onto Greens Point Rd where the light is found in 1.5 km

Coordinates: 45°02'20.0"N 66°53'31.0"W

Opened: 1903

Automated: 1996

Deactivated: Active

Height: 12 meters, 39 feet

Focal Height: 17 meters, 56 feet

Signal: Fixed white

Foghorn Signal: 1 blast every 30 seconds

Visitor Access: Closed

Grindstone Island Lighthouse

The original Grindstone Island Lighthouse opened in 1859 as an aid to ships entering Shepody Bay. A fog alarm was added to the station in 1877 with a new landing platform as well. The island is a protected area for breeding birds and in 2010, the Grindstone Island Nature Preserve was created.

Description: White, hexagonal concrete tower

Location: Harvey Bank

Directions: Accessible by boat

Coordinates: 45°43'19.0"N 64°37'15.0"W

Opened: 1911

Automated: 1970

Deactivated: 2001

Height: 21 meters, 68 feet

Focal Height: 18 meters, 59 feet

Signal: Not known

Foghorn signal: Not known

Visitor Access: Closed

Hampstead Wharf Lighthouse

The Hampstead Wharf Lighthouse was erected to guide ships to the Hampstead Wharf. The contract to build it was fulfilled by G.W. Palmer. The Saint John River Society acquired the lighthouse in 2009 and restored it in 2010.

Description: White, square wooden tower

Location: Hampstead

Directions: From Hampstead, head NW on NB-102 N and the lighthouse is 300 meters

Coordinates: 45°37'30.0"N 66°05'05.0"W

Opened: 1912

Automated: 1912

Deactivated: 1994

Height: 8 meters, 27 feet

Focal Height: 11 meters, 36 feet

Signal: Fixed white

Foghorn signal: N/A

Visitor Access: Grounds open, tower closed

Head Harbour (East Quoddy) Lighthouse

The New Brunswick Government budged funds to build the Head Harbour (East Quoddy) Lighthouse in 1829 and it opened that same year. It is the second oldest New Brunswick light station. A fog horn was added in 1880 and a third-order Fresnel lens was installed in 1887.

Description: White octagonal tower

Location: Wilson's Beach

Directions: Accessible by boat

Coordinates: 44°57'28"N 66°54'00"W

Opened: 1829

Automated: 1986

Deactivated: Active

Height: 15.5 meters, 51 feet

Focal Height: 17.5 meters, 57 feet

Signal: Fixed red

Foghorn Signal: 1 blast every minute

Visitor Access: Grounds open, tower closed

Hendry Farm Lighthouse

The original Hendry Farm Lighthouse opened in 1876 to aid ships travelling to the entrance to Washademoak Lake. They were erected by J.C & J.Q. Wetmore. By 1892, inspection showed the site in poor condition and a new tower opened in 1896. The lighthouse was decommissioned in 1995.

Description: Square wooden tower

Location: Lower Cambridge

Directions: 59 Washademoak Lane, Cambridge-Narrows

Coordinates: 45°43'59.0"N 66°02'54.0"W

Opened: 1896

Automated: 1936

Deactivated: 1995

Height: 8 meters, 27 feet

Focal Height: 9 meters, 30 feet

Signal: Fixed white

Foghorn Signal: N/A

Visitor Access: Grounds open, tower closed

Inch Arran Point Range Lights

Front Range

Inch Arran Point is the northernmost point in New Brunswick and in 1970 a lighthouse was erected there to warn ships of the Bon Ami Rocks. It became a front range light when a skeleton tower was erected at the west. Inch Arran Lighthouse was recognized as a Federal Heritage Building on September 5, 1991

Front Range

Description: Square wooden Tower

Location: Dalhousie

Directions: From Dalhousie, head east on Victoria St for 1.4 km and see the light

Coordinates: 48°03'40.0"N 66°21'03.0"W

Opened: 1870

Automated: 1997

Deactivated: Active

Height: 11 meters, 36 feet

Focal Height: 14 meters, 45 feet

Signal: White flash every 6 seconds

Visitor Access: Grounds open, tower closed

Rear Range

Description: Skeleton tower

Location: Dalhousie

Directions: From Dalhousie, head east on Victoria St for 1 km and see the light

Coordinates: 48°03'42.6"N 66°21'20.3"W

Opened: 1972

Automated: 1972

Deactivated: Active

Height: 11 meters, 36 feet

Focal Height: 14 meters, 45 feet

Signal: White flash every 6 seconds

Visitor Access: Closed

Leonardville Lighthouse

Leonardville Lighthouse, a white square tower, was built on the top of a cliff on the eastern shore of Deer Island in 1913 under contract by A.L. Mury. It is an aid to mariners looking to enter Leonardville Harbor from the west. It continues to be active.

Description: White square tower

Location: Leonardville

Directions: From Leonardville, head SE on NB-772 for 850 meters and find the light

Coordinates: 44°58'06"N 66°57'18"W

Opened: 1914

Automated: 1936

Deactivated: Active

Height: 9 meters, 29 feet

Focal Height: 20 meters, 66 feet

Signal: Fixed white

Foghorn signal: N/A

Visitor Access: Closed

Lighthouse Point Lighthouse

The original Lighthouse Point Lighthouse was built in 1876 by W. B. Deacon and John Ward. The lighthouse served to aid ships travelling into Beaver Harbour. In 1900, a hand foghorn was added to the site. The current tower opened in 1983 and is still active.

Description: White cylindrical tower

Location: Beaver Harbour

Directions: From Beaver Harbour, head SE on Main St/NB-778 for 1.0 km and turn left on Lighthouse Rd where the light is 800 meters

Coordinates: 45°03'47.0"N 66°43'59.0"W

Opened: 1984

Automated: 1984

Deactivated: Active

Height: 8 meters, 26 feet

Focal Height: 14 meters meters, 47 feet

Signal: White flash every 6 seconds

Foghorn signal: 1 blast every 60 seconds

Visitor Access: Grounds open, tower closed

Long Eddy Point Lighthouse

A fog signal was established here in 1874 and operated for over 90 years before the Long Eddy Point Lighthouse was built in 1966. It sends a red flashing light and is still active. Long Eddy Point Lighthouse was listed as a heritage lighthouse 2017.

Description: White rectangular tower

Location: North Head

Directions: From Rocky Corner, head NW on Whistle Rd for 3.5 km and the light

Coordinates: 44°47'59.0"N 66°47'08.0"W

Opened: 1966

Automated: 1989

Deactivated: Active

Height: 9 meters, 31 feet

Focal Height: 39 meters, 127 feet

Signal: Red flash every 8 seconds

Foghorn Signal: 1 blast every 60 seconds

Visitor Access: Grounds open, tower closed

Long Point Lighthouse

This site on White Head Island started as a fog signal station which was built in 1929 by G. Stephen Whitehead. In 1966, the Long Point Lighthouse was built as well as a new fog alarm building. The site remains active.

Description: White rectangular tower

Location: White Head Island

Directions: Accessible by boat

Coordinates: 44°36'50.0"N 66°42'35.0"W

Opened: 1966

Automated: 1984

Deactivated: Active

Height: 9 meters, 31 feet

Focal Height: 58 meters, 58 feet

Signal: White flash every 12 seconds

Foghorn Signal: Blast every 20 seconds

Visitor Access: Grounds open, tower closed

Lower Musquash Island Light

In 1876, a pair of range light were built to mark the way into to Washademoak Lake. One was placed at Lower Musquash Island and the other at Hendry Farm. They were erected by J.C & J.Q. Wetmore. The present tower was built in 1924. It was deactivated in 1994.

Description: White, square pyramidal wooden tower

Location: Entrance to Washademoak Lake

Directions: Accessible by boat

Coordinates: 45°42'29.0"N 66°03'58.0"W

Opened: 1924

Automated: Not known

Deactivated: 1994

Height: 11 meters, 37 feet

Focal Height: 12 meters, 40 feet

Signal: Not known

Foghorn Signal: N/A

Visitor Access: Closed

Lower Neguac Wharf Range Rear Light

A series of islands range in front of the entrance to Miramichi Bay. In 1873, Neguac Lighthouse was built on the Neguac Sandbar, to guide vessels through Neguac Gully. It was automated in 1957 and deactivated in 2003.

Description: White, square, pyramidal wooden tower

Location: Neguac

Directions: From Lower Neguac, head south on Rue Godin for 800 meters to find the light

Coordinates: 47°15'41.0"N 65°03'13.0"W

Opened: 1892

Automated: 1957

Deactivated: 2003

Height: 9 meters, 28 feet

Focal Height: 11 meters, 35 feet

Signal: Fixed white

Foghorn signal: N/A

Visitor Access: Closed

Machias Seal Island Lighthouse

Machias Seal Island is equidistant from Canada and the united States and this has been the root of a dispute over sovereignty. Canada has built and maintained the lighthouse and has continued to staff it with keepers, as well as as a warden to regulates visitors who come to see puffins. As this is a prime fishing grounds, the United States continues to maintain its sovereignty as well. In 1832 two wooden towers were built on the island. As the area is often in fog, a signal gun was added in 1841. In 1856-1857, the station underwent repairs to both the towers and dwelling. A replacement for one of the towers opened in 1878 and a fog alarm was added in 1914. The current tower replaced the two existing in 1915.

Description: Tapered octagonal tower

Location: Machias Seal Island

Directions: Accessible by boat

Coordinates: 44°30'06.6"N 67°06'04.1"W

Opened: 1915

Automated: Not automated

Deactivated: Active

Height: 18 meters, 60 feet

Focal Height: 25 meters, 83 feet

Signal: Flashing white

Foghorn Signal: One 2 second blast every 15 seconds

Visitor Access: Grounds open, tower closed

McColgan Point Lighthouse

The McColgan Point Lighthouse was built in 1914 by B.R. Palmer to aid ships travelling the narrow channel that runs between Kennebecasis Island and the Kingston Peninsula. It was originally equipped with a sixth-order dioptric lens. McColgan Point Lighthouse and Bayswater Lighthouse were the last two lights to be built along the St. John River.

Description: White square tower

Location: Summerville

Directions: From the Kennebesasis Island Ferry Terminal, head north on unnamed road for 500 meters to see the lighthouse

Coordinates: 45°19'56"N 66°06'34"W

Opened: 1914

Automated: Not known

Deactivated: Active

Height: 8 meters, 27 feet

Focal Height: 11 meters, 37 feet

Signal: White flash every 12 seconds

Foghorn signal: N/A

Visitor Access: Grounds open, tower closed

Miscou Island Lighthouse

The Miscou Island Lighthouse was built by James Murray and opened in 1856. It was equipped with a revolving Fresnel lens and is the only New Brunswick lighthouse with that type of lens still in place. A fog alarm building was added in 1874. The station is listed as a Federal Heritage Building.

Description: White octagonal tower

Location: Miscou Island

Directions: From Miscou, head east on New Brunswick 113 N for 1.8 km to find the site

Coordinates: 48°00'34.0"N 64°29'35.0"W

Opened: 1856

Automated: 1988

Deactivated: Active

Height: 25 meters, 83 feet

Focal Height: 24 meters, 80 feet

Signal: Green flash every 5 seconds

Foghorn Signal: Blast every 30 seconds

Visitor Access: Grounds open, tower open in summer

Mulholland Point Lighthouse

The Mulholland Point Lighthouse was built in 1885 to guide ships through the Lubec Narrows. The lighthouse was deactivated with the completion of the Franklin D. Roosevelt Bridge and the lighthouse became part of Roosevelt Campobello International Park.

Description: White, octagonal wooden tower

Location: Welshpool

Directions: From Welshpool, head south on NB-774 S for 2.5 km and make a slight right onto Narrows Rd. After 0.3 km find the light

Coordinates: 44°51'47.0"N 66°58'47.0"W

Opened: 1885

Automated: Not known

Deactivated: 1963

Height: 14 meters, 46 feet

Focal Height: 18 meters, 60 feet

Signal: White fixed

Foghorn signal: N/A

Visitor Access: Grounds open, tower closed

Musquash Head Lighthouse

The original Musquash Head Lighthouse was a wooden tower built in 1879. It was replaced by the present tower in 1959. In 1967 a fog horn was added to the site. The lighthouse was automated in the 1980s and continues to be active.

Description: White, hexagonal concrete tower

Location: Lorneville

Directions: Coastal trail

Coordinates: 45°08'37.0"N 66°14'14.0"W

Opened: 1959

Automated: 1987

Deactivated: Active

Height: 14 meters, 46 feet

Focal Height: 35 meters, 115 feet

Signal: White flash every 3 seconds

Foghorn signal: 1 blast every 60 seconds

Visitor Access: Grounds open, tower closed

Oak Point Lighthouse

Oak Point is at the north end of Long Reach on the Saint John River and there are several islands in the area which present hazards to ships, In 1869 a series of 6 lights were erected by John Duffy including the Oak Point Lighthouse. In 1902 the current tower with a stronger light replaced the original.

Description: White square tower

Location: Oak Point

Directions: From Oak Point, head SE on Oak Point Beach Rd for 450 m and turn left to continue onto Oak Point Beach Rd and the lighthouse

Coordinates: 45°30'27.0"N 66°04'48.0"W

Opened: 1902

Automated: 1923

Deactivated: Active

Height: 15 meters, 48 feet

Focal Height: 16 meters, 52 feet

Signal: Green flash every 10 seconds

Foghorn signal: N/A

Visitor Access: Grounds open, tower closed

Oak Point Range Front Lighthouse

In 1904 a pair of range lights were built at Oak Point by R. A. Russell. They replaced lanterns fixed from masts. The lights were deactivated in 1952 and the Front Range Light was moved to its present position on private property.

Description: White, square wooden tower

Location: Moorefield

Directions: From Moorefield, head northeast on NB-11 for 900 m and the light can be seen from the road

Coordinates: 47°03'03.0"N 65°28'06.0"W

Opened: 1904

Automated: N/A

Deactivated: 1952

Height: 16 meters, 53 feet

Focal Height: 18 meters, 60 feet

Signal: Fixed white

Foghorn signal: N/A

Visitor Access: Closed (Visible from public road)

Partridge Island Lighthouse

The first light on Partridge Island opened in 1791, built to guide ships into Saint John Harbour. It was New Brunswick's first lighthouse. A fog bell was added to the station in 1831. The tower was lost to an 1832 fire but was quickly rebuilt. The current lighthouse replaced it in 1959.

Description: Octagonal concrete tower

Location: Saint John

Directions: Visible from the Saint John waterfront and the Saint John - Digby ferry

Coordinates: 45°14'21.0"N 66°03'14.0"W

Opened: 1959

Automated: 1980

Deactivated: Active

Height: 14 meters, 45 feet

Focal Height: 35 meters, 115 feet

Signal: White flash every 7.5 seconds

Foghorn Signal: 2 blasts every 30 seconds

Visitor Access: Closed

Pea Point Lighthouse

The original Pea Point Lighthouse opened in 1878 at the eastern entrance to L'Etang Harbour. It had a signal of fixed green but was changed to fixed white in 1914. A fog horn was added to the site in 1900 and in 1929 it was upgraded with a fog alarm building. In 1965 the present concrete lighthouse opened and is active today.

Description: White rectangular tower

Location: Blacks Harbour

Directions: Visible from Grand Manan Ferry

Coordinates: 45°02'21"N 66°48'28"W

Opened: 1965

Automated: 1967

Deactivated: Active

Height: 11 meters, 35 feet

Focal Height: 17 meters, 56 feet

Signal: Fixed white

Foghorn signal: 2 blasts every 60 seconds

Visitor Access: Grounds open, tower closed

Pecks Point Lighthouse

In 1889 a lighthouse was built by George Ingram at Ward's Point to aid ships travelling the Cumberland Basin. In 1908 the light was relocated to Peck's Point as it was deemed to be more useful there. A fog alarm building was added the following year. The tower was sold into private hands in the 1970s.

Description: Square Pyramidal Tower

Location: Upper Rockport

Directions: From Upper Rockport, head SW on Lower Rockport Rd for 450 m and the lighthouse is by the road

Coordinates: 45°45'33.8"N 64°29'19.9"W

Opened: 1908

Automated: Not known

Deactivated: 1970s

Height: 7 meters, 22 feet

Focal Height: 25 meters, 81 feet

Signal: Fixed white

Foghorn Signal: Not known

Visitor Access: Closed

Point Escuminac Lighthouse

Point Escuminac Lighthouse opened in 18421 as an aid to mariners at the northern entrance to the Northumberland Strait. It was the first light on New Brunswick's northern coast. The lighting was updated to a third-order French Fresnel lens in 1869. In 1874 a fog horn was added to the site. The current tower replaced the original in 1966.

Description: White hexagonal tower

Location: Escuminac

Directions: From Escuminac, head NE on Escuminac Point Rd for 9.4 km and the site

Coordinates: 47°04'23.0"N 64°47'53.0"W

Opened: 1963

Automated: 1989

Deactivated: Active

Height: 13 meters, 43 feet

Focal Height: 21 meters, 68 feet

Signal: White flash every 3 seconds

Foghorn signal: 2 blasts every 60 seconds

Visitor Access: Grounds open, tower closed

Point Lepreau Lighthouse

The original Point Lepreau Lighthouse was opened in 1831 to warn ships of Point Lepreau which projects into the Bay of Fundy. The lighthouse was distinctive as it had an upper and lower light. A fog alarm was added in 1869. In 1898 the lighthouse was destroyed in a fire. A new tower opened in 1899 but it was destroyed by lightning in 1956. The present tower opened in 1958. The Point Lepreau Nuclear Plant opened at the site in 1983 and permission is needed to visit the site.

Description: Octagonal tower, red and white horizontal bands

Location: Dipper Harbour

Directions: Permission needed

Coordinates: 45°03'32"N 66°27'31"W

Opened: 1959

Automated: 1980

Deactivated: Active

Height: 17 meters, 58 feet

Focal Height: 25 meters, 84 feet

Signal: White flash every 3 seconds

Foghorn signal: 3 blasts every 60 seconds

Visitor Access: Closed

Pointe à Brideau Range Rear Lighthouse

A pair of skeleton towers were established at Pointe à Brideau in 1978. The town of Caraquet was looking to improve their beach area near the Rear Range Light and received permission from the Canadian Coast Guard to build a wooden tower around the skeleton tower and it was completed in 1991.

Description: Square pyramidal wood tower

Location: Caraquet

Directions: From Caraquet head north off NB-145 on Rue Foley for 350 meters to the lighthouse

Coordinates: 47°47'42.2"N 64°56'29.8"W

Opened: 1978

Automated: 1978

Deactivated: 2020

Height: 15 meters, 50 feet

Focal Height: 19 meters, 64 feet

Signal: Fixed red

Foghorn signal: N/A

Visitor Access: Grounds open, tower closed

Pointe à Jérôme Range Front Lighthouse

In 1883 a set of range lights was constructed at Pointe à Jérôme to aid vessels to the entrance of Bouctouche Harbour. The range lights were deactivated in 2014. Pointe à Jérôme Rear Range Lighthouse was demolished in 2022 while the surviving Front Range received a Heritage designation the same year.

Description: White square tower

Location: Bouctouche

Directions: From Baie de Bouctouche, head south on NB-475 S for 1.7 km and find the site

Coordinates: 46°29'12.0"N 64°40'46.0"W

Opened: 1916

Automated: 1963

Deactivated: 2014

Height: 4 meters, 14 feet

Focal Height: 6 meters, 19 feet

Signal: Fixed red

Foghorn Signal: N/A

Visitor Access: Grounds open, tower closed

Pointe du Chêne Range Lights

By the 1850s the harbour at Shediac Bay was becoming busy with fishing and lumber. Temporary range lights of lanterns on top of masts were established in 1895. In 1898, wooden towers were erected to replace them. Both lights were deactivated in 2020. They underwent restoration in 2017.

Front Range

Description: Square Pyramidal Tower

Location: Pointe du Chêne

Directions: 221 Parlee Beach Rd
Pointe-du-Chêne

Coordinates: 46°14'27.0"N 64°30'42.0"W

Opened: 1898

Automated: Not known

Deactivated: 2020

Height: 8 meters, 27 feet

Focal Height: 8 meters, 26 feet

Signal: Fixed Red

Visitor Access: Grounds open, tower closed

Rear Range

Description: Square Pyramidal Tower

Location: Pointe du Chêne

Directions: 24 Parlee Beach Rd
Pointe-du-Chêne

Coordinates: 46°14'22.0"N 64°30'43.0"W

Opened: 1898

Automated: Not known

Deactivated: 2020

Height: 12 meters, 39 feet

Height: 14 meters, 45 feet

Signal: Fixed Red

Visitor Access: Grounds open, tower closed

Pointe Sapin Range Rear Lighthouse

The Pointe Sapin Range Rear Lighthouse was established in 1910, primarily as an aid to local fishermen. It was built by James Legoof. It replaced a pole light which had operated from 1903. The new tower had a a sixth-order lens installed to upgrade the lighting equipment.

Description: White, square, pyramidal wooden tower

Location: Pointe Sapin

Directions: From Pointe-Sapin Centre, head northeast on NB-117 N for 2.3 km and find the lighthouse.

Coordinates: 46°57'50.0"N 64°49'50.0"W

Opened: 1910

Automated: 1959

Deactivated: Active

Height: 8 meters, 25 feet

Focal Height: 11 meters, 37 feet

Signal: Fixed white

Foghorn signal: N/A

Visitor Access: Grounds open, tower closed

Portage Island Range Rear Lighthouse

In 1869, the Portage Island Range Rear Lighthouse was originally erected on the southern tip of Portage Island as an aid to ships entering Inner Miramichi Bay. The lantern room was built from old portions from Point Escuminac Lighthouse. A breakwater was put added in 1883 to prevent the sea from eroding the station. The lighthouse was deactivated in 1986 and was moved to its present location as part of the New Brunswick Aquarium and Marine Centre.

Description: Square pyramidal tower

Location: Shippigan

Directions: In Shippagan, head NW on Rue de Grâcefrom NB-113 and find the light in 400 meters

Coordinates: 47°44'53.0"N 64°42'33.0"W

Opened: 1908

Automated: 1961

Deactivated: 1986

Height: 13 meters, 42 feet

Focal Height: 15 meters, 48 feet

Signal: White flash every 4 seconds

Foghorn Signal: N/A

Visitor Access: Grounds open, tower closed

Quaco Head Lighthouse

The first Quaco Head Lighthouse was an octagonal tower which was erected in 1835. Its lighting equipment involved a revolving lights powered by weights which needed to be wound every four hours. In 1848 the tower was raised 30 feet with the lighting upgraded. The station was destroyed in a fire in 1881 and a replacement was opened in 1883. The present tower opened in 1966.

Description: White tower

Location: West Quaco

Directions: From West Quaco, head SW on W Quaco Rd for 1.7 km and turn left onto Lighthouse Rd where the site is 1.2 km.

Coordinates: 45°19'26.0"N 65°32'07.0"W

Opened: 1976

Automated: 1987

Deactivated: Active

Height: 12 meters, 38 feet

Focal Height: 26 meters, 85

Signal: White flash every 10 seconds

Foghorn Signal: Blast every 30 seconds

Visitor Access: Grounds open, tower closed

Reed's Point Light

Although it is not actually a lighthouse, it is included here as an interesting historical navigation aid. The three lamps shine red towards the sea and white towards the shore. It was raised 15 feet in 1897 to make it more noticeable. It is popularly known locally as the Three Sisters Lamps.

Description: Trident on pole

Location: Saint John

Directions: Prince William St, Saint John

Coordinates: 45°16'01.7"N 66°03'37.5"W

Opened: 1848

Automated: 1848

Deactivated: 1997

Height: 8 meters, 27 feet

Focal Height: 13 meters, 42 feet

Signal: Fixed red/white

Foghorn signal: N/A

Visitor Access: Grounds open

Renforth Lighthouse

The Renforth Lighthouse was built in the 1980s as a private navigational aid by the Renforth Boat Club. The name is said to refer to James Renforth, a rower who died of a heart attack while competing on the Kennebecasis River in 1870.

Description: Square pyramidal tower

Location: Saint John

Directions: 141 James Renforth Dr, Rothesay

Coordinates: 45°21'27.6"N 66°00'51.8"W

Opened: 1980s

Automated: 1980s

Deactivated: Active

Height: 6 meters, 20 feet

Focal Height: Not known

Signal: Fixed white

Foghorn signal: N/A

Visitor Access: Grounds open, tower closed

Richibucto Head (Cap Lumière) Lighthouse

The original Richibucto Head Lighthouse was erected in 1865 by Amos Keith. It was equipped with a 4th order Fresnel lens, at that time state of the art. It was replaced by the current tower in 1901 and it is still active.

Description: White square tower

Location: Cap Lumière

Directions: From Cap Lumiere, head north on Cap Lumière Rd for 1.1 km and the lighthouse is by the roadside

Coordinates: 46°40'11.0"N 64°42'42.0"W

Opened: 1901

Automated: 1965

Deactivated: Active

Height: 10 meters, 33 feet

Focal Height: 18 meters, 59 feet

Signal: White flash every 5 seconds

Foghorn signal: N/A

Visitor Access: Grounds open, tower closed

Robertson Point Lighthouse

Charles Macpherson built the original Robertson Point Lighthouse which was first lit in 1873. The site was upgraded with a 7th order lens in 1905. The light was replaced by a white cylindrical fiberglass tower at an unknown time.

Description: White cylindrical tower

Location: Whites Cove

Directions: From Whites Cove, head SW on Rte 105 N/NB-105 N for 3.8 km and turn right onto Robertson Point Rd and the site is 1.1 km

Coordinates: 45°52'19.9"N 66°06'10.8"W

Opened: Not known

Automated: Not known

Deactivated: Active

Height: 8 meters, 25 feet

Focal Height: 12 meters, 40 feet

Signal: Red flash every 4 seconds

Foghorn signal: N/A

Visitor Access: Grounds open, tower closed

Sand Point Lighthouse

In 1869, six beacon lights were put into operation on the Saint John River to support the steamships travelling between Saint John and Fredericton. This included a light at Sand Point. Ships going upstream from Saint John steer directly towards the light to find the course to the upper river. The site was listed as a Heritage site in 2016 and is still active.

Description: Skeleton tower

Location: Sand Point

Directions: From Sand Point, head south on Sand Point Wharf Rd for 260 meters and turn left onto Old Path Ln and the site

Coordinates: 45°20'33.0"N 66°11'56.0"W

Opened: 1869

Automated: 1869

Deactivated: Active

Height: 18 meters, 58 feet

Focal Height: 23 meters, 75 feet

Signal: Fixed red

Foghorn signal: N/A

Visitor Access: Grounds open, tower closed

Southwest Head Lighthouse

In 1880, B. J. Austin built the Southwest Head Lighthouse which was to aid ships travelling the North Channel of the Bay of Fundy. In 1900, a hand foghorn was added to the station. In 1958, the current tower replaced the original which was demolished. The light was automated in 1987.

Description: Square white tower

Location: Seal Cove

Directions: From Deep Cove, head southwest on NB-776 S/Rte 776 for 4.5 km and find the light.

Coordinates: 44°36'04"N 66°54'20"W

Opened: 1959

Automated: 1987

Deactivated: Active

Height: 10 meters, 33 feet

Focal Height: 48 meters, 157 feet

Signal: White flash every 10 seconds

Foghorn signal: Blast every 60 seconds

Visitor Access: Grounds open, tower closed

Southwest Wolf Island Lighthouse

The original Southwest Wolf Island Lighthouse was erected in 1971. It consisted of a square tower built onto the keeper's dwelling. In 1900 the site had a fog horn added and in 1905 the lighting was upgraded with a 3rd order lens. The current fiberglass tower was opened in 1982 and is still active.

Description: White cylindrical tower

Location: Otter Cove

Directions: Accessible by boat

Coordinates: 44°56'12.0"N 66°44'00.0"W

Opened: 1982

Automated: 1982

Deactivated: Active

Height: 11 meters, 36 feet

Focal Height: 38 meters, 125 feet

Signal: White flash every 10 seconds

Foghorn signal: Hand fog horn

Visitor Access: Grounds open, tower closed

St. Andrews North Point (Pendlebury) Lighthouse

Built in 1833, the St. Andrews Lighthouse is the oldest surviving mainland light in New Brunswick. It is also called the Pendlebury Lighthouse for the family who served as keepers for almost a century. The light served ships entering the St. Andrews harbour. In 2010 the tower received an extensive restoration.

Description: White, octagonal wooden tower

Location: St. Andrews

Directions: End of Patrick Street in St. Andrews

Coordinates: 45°04'03.0"N 67°02'50.0"W

Opened: 1833

Automated: N/A

Deactivated: 1938

Height: 7 meters, 23 feet

Focal Height: 9 meters, 30 feet

Signal: Red flash every 4 seconds

Foghorn Signal: N/A

Visitor Access: Grounds open, tower closed

St Martins Lighthouse

The St Martins Lighthouse is a replica of the Quaco Head Lighthouse, although smaller in size. Note that there are two historic Covered Bridges nearby. The structure is a tourist information center for the St. Martins area in summer.

Description: White, square wooden tower

Location: St Martins

Directions: From St. Martins, head NW on Main St for 2.2 km and the site

Coordinates: 45°21'34.9"N 65°31'57.4"W

Opened: 1983

Automated: N/A

Deactivated: N/A

Height: 7 meters, 22 feet

Focal Height: 9 meters, 30 feet

Signal: Fixed red light

Foghorn Signal: N/A

Visitor Access: Grounds open, tower open seasonally

Swallowtail Lighthouse

In 1857, the ship Lord Ashburton wrecked on the northern shore of Grand Manan with the loss of 21 lives. This disaster prompted calls for a lighthouse in that area. Plans for the Swallowtail Lighthouse were prepared and John P. McKay fulfilled the contract with the station opening in 1860. The light was fixed white but in 1907 the lighting was upgraded to a 4th order lens and was changed to occulting white. The station was automated in 1986 and is still active.

Description: White octagonal tower

Location: North Head

Directions: From Tattons Corner, head east on NB-776 N/Rte 776 for 350 meters and continue onto Pettes Cove Rd. for 140 meters and turn left onto Old Airport Rd, then right onto Lighthouse Rd and the lighthouse

Coordinates: 44°45'52"N 66°43'57"W

Opened: 1860

Automated: 1986

Deactivated: Active

Height: 16 meters, 53 feet

Focal Height: 37 meters, 122 feet

Signal: White flash every 6 seconds

Foghorn Signal: Blast every 20 seconds

Visitor Access: Grounds open, tower opened occasionally

Swift Point (Green Head) Lighthouse

The Swift Point Lighthouse was one of 6 opened along the Saint John River in 1869. In 1896 this tower was replaced with a new tower built by Mr. G. W. Palmer which showed a fixed white signal. In 1914 a fog bell was added. On June 13, 2017, this tower was destroyed by fire. The Canadian Coast Guard quickly replaced it and it opened in 2018.

Description: White pyramid tower

Location: Randolph

Directions: From Randolph, head NW on Green Head Road to Quarry Road and proceed to a gated road and park. Walk the trail north for 1.1 km and the light.

Coordinates: 45°16'57.0"N 66°07'17.0"W

Opened: 2018

Automated: 2018

Deactivated: Active

Height: 14 meters, 46 feet

Focal Height: 28 meters, 92 feet

Signal: Green flash every 4 seconds

Foghorn signal: N/A

Visitor Access: Grounds open, tower closed

The Cedars Lighthouse

In the 1900s, The Cedars became a popular destination for tourists who would take a riverboat on the Saint John River to a large hotel. The Cedars Lighthouse was erected in 1904 near the hotel to guide these riverboats. In 2005 the Kingston Peninsula Heritage society assumed management of the site. In 2008 a walking path was completed for those wishing to view the light.

Description: White, square pyramidal wooden tower

Location: The Cedars

Directions: From The Cedars, head SW on NB-845 W for 180 meters and turn right onto Maple Grove Ln to see the lighthouse

Coordinates: 45°28'42.0"N 66°04'57.0"W

Opened: 1904

Automated: Not known

Deactivated: 1994

Height: 10 meters, 32 feet

Focal Height: 13 meters, 44 feet

Signal: Fixed red

Foghorn signal: N/A

Visitor Access: Grounds open, tower closed

Wilmot Bluff Lighthouse

In 1869, six lighthouses were opened on the Saint John River to aid ships travelling between Fredericton and Saint John. This included the Wilmot Bluff Light which was a lantern on a mast. They were built by John Duffy. They were later replaced by enclosed structures with Wilmot Bluff Lighthouse completed in 1908. The structure was sold into private hands in 1969.

Description: White, square, wooden tower

Location: Oromocto

Directions: From Lower Lincoln, head east on Thatch Rd for 190 meters. Private property but viewable from public road

Coordinates: 45°52'09.0"N 66°30'38.0"W

Opened: 1908

Automated: N/A

Deactivated: 1967

Height: 13 meters, 42 feet

Focal Height: 30 meters, 100 feet

Signal: Fixed white

Foghorn signal: N/A

Visitor Access: Closed

Tours

Bay of Fundy Tour

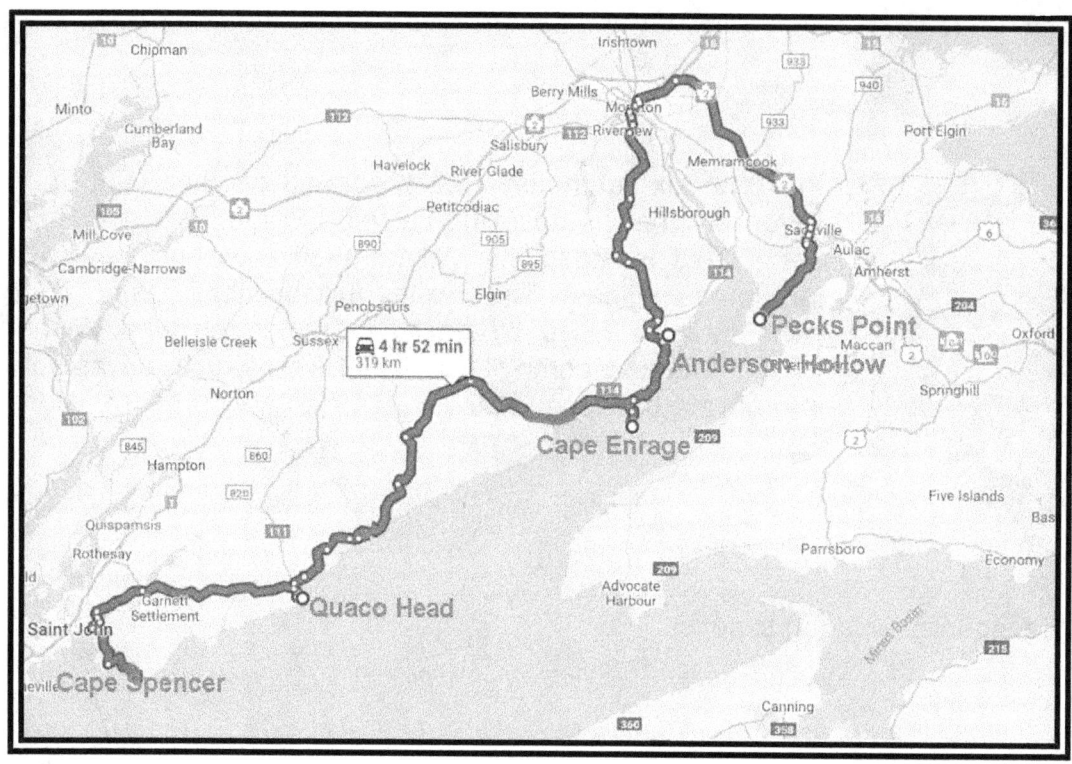

4 Lighthouses 5 hours driving

Pecks Point	45°45'33.8"N 64°29'19.9"W
Anderson Hollow	45°44'06.7"N 64°41'50.2"W
Cape Enrage	45°35'38.0"N 64°46'48.0"W
Quaco Head	45°19'26.0"N 65°32'07.0"W
Cape Spencer	45°11'42.9"N 65°54'35.5"W

Miramichi Tour

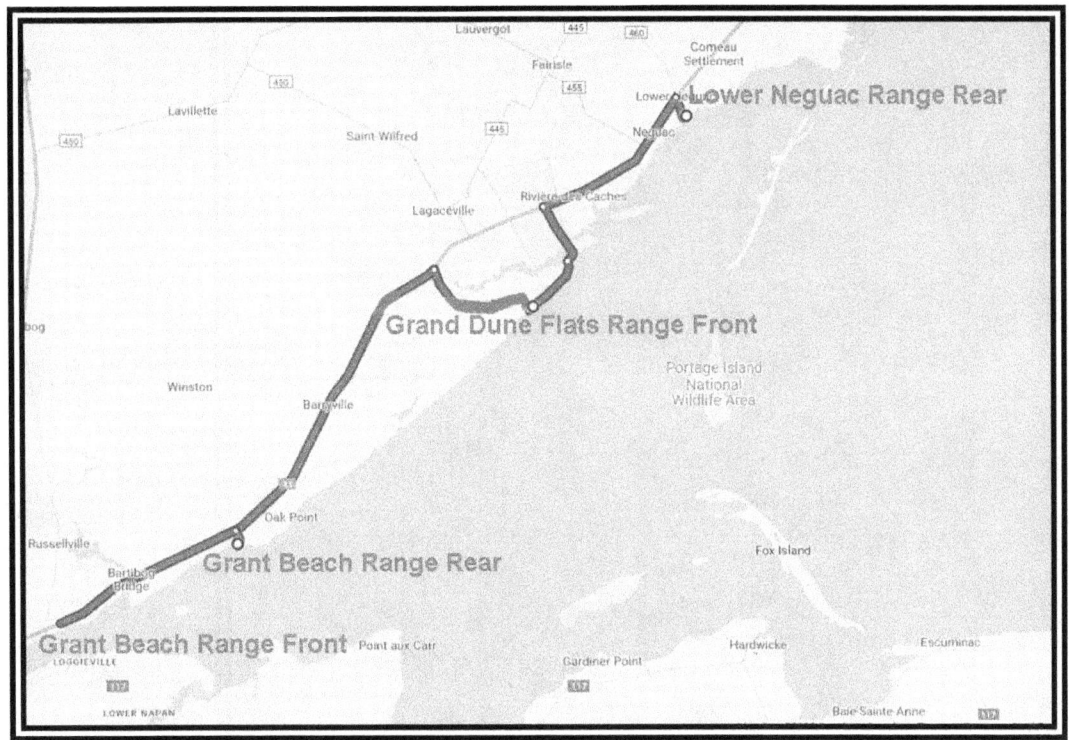

4 Lighthouses 45 minutes driving

Lower Neguac Range Rear	47°15'41.0"N 65°03'13.0"W
Grand Dune Flats Range Front	47°11'41.0"N 65°08'07.0"W
Grant Beach Range Rear	47°06'43.0"N 65°17'31.0"W
Grant Beach Range Front	47°05'07.0"N 65°23'11.0"W

Northumberland Strait Tour

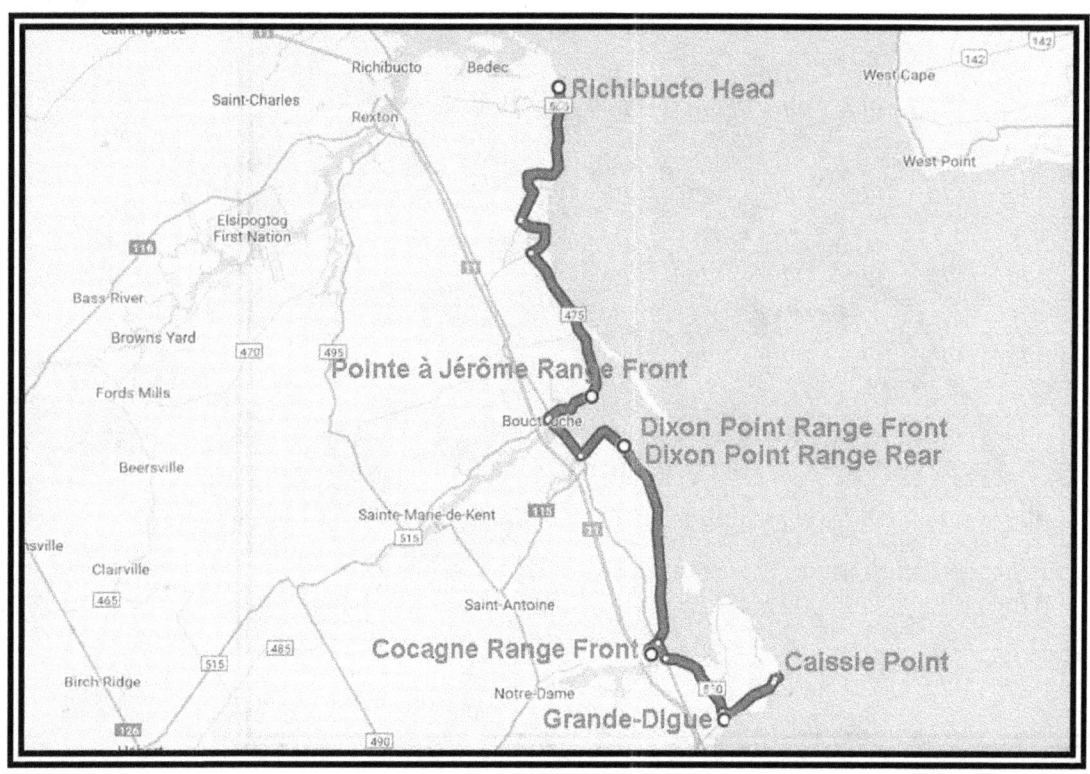

7 lighthouses 1 hour 15 minutes driving

Richibucto Head	46°40'11.0"N 64°42'42.0"W
Pointe à Jérôme Range Front	46°29'12.0"N 64°40'46.0"W
Dixon Point Range Front	46°27'24.0"N 64°39'03.0"W
Dixon Point Range Rear	46°27'24.0"N 64°39'03.0"W
Cocagne Range Front	46°20'01.1"N 64°37'32.4"W
Grande-Digue	46°17'41.0"N 64°33'38.0"W
Caissie Point	46°19'11.4"N 64°30'45.5"W

St Lawrence River Tour

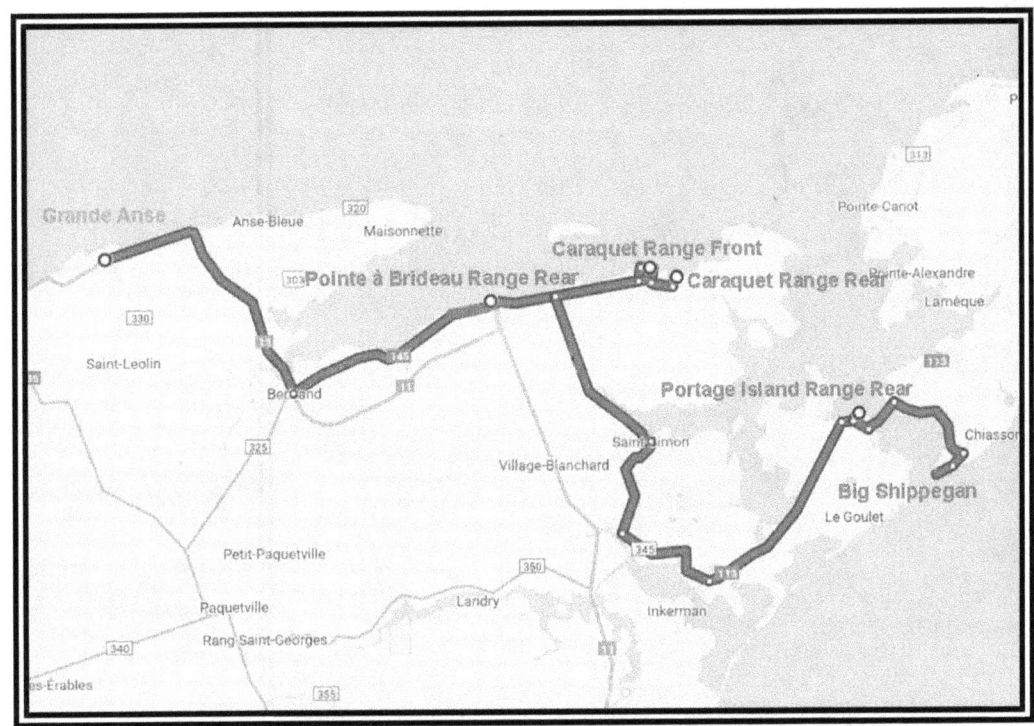

6 lighthouses 1 hour 30 minutes driving

Grande Anse	47°48'44.4"N 65°11'06.7"W
Pointe à Brideau Range Rear	47°47'42.2"N 64°56'29.8"W
Caraquet Range Front	47°48'29.8"N 64°50'27.9"W
Caraquet Range Rear	47°48'16.0"N 64°49'29.0"W
Portage Island Range Rear	47°44'53.0"N 64°42'33.0"W
Big Shippegan	47°43'20.0"N 64°39'38.0"W

Saint John River

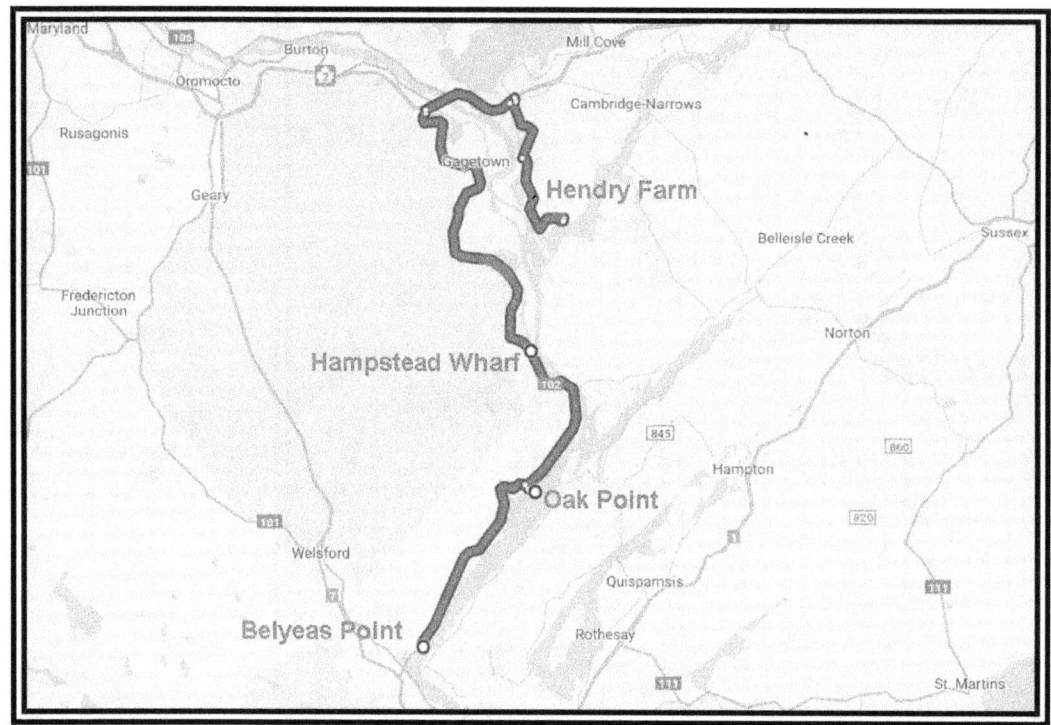

4 lighthouses 1 hour 30 minutes driving

Belyeas Point	45°22'41.0"N 66°12'58.0"W
Oak Point	45°30'27.0"N 66°04'48.0"W
Hampstead Wharf	45°37'30.0"N 66°05'05.0"W
Hendry Farm	45°43'59.0"N 66°02'54.0"W

Glossary of Lighthouse Terms

Aerobeacon: A lighting system which creates a signal over long distances. It consists of a strong light source with a focusing mechanism which is rotated on a vertical axis. It has been used at airports as well as lighthouses.

Acetylene: After 1910, acetylene began to be used to power the lighthouse light source. It has the advantage that it could be stored on site with a sun valve turning it on at dusk and off at daybreak.

Alternating Light: A light source which changes colours in a regular pattern.

Arc of Visibility: The range of the horizon from which the lighthouse is visible from the sea.

Automated: A lighthouse that operates without a keeper. The light functions are controlled by timers, and light and fog detectors.

Beacon: A fixed aid to navigation.

Bell: A sound signal produced by fixed aids and by sea movement on buoys.

Breakwater: A structure that protects a shore area or harbour by blocking waves.

Bull's-eye Lens: A convex lens used to refract light.

Catwalk: An elevated walkway which allows the keeper to move in the lantern room in towers built in the sea.

Characteristic: The distinct pattern of the flashing light or foghorn blast which allows seamen to distinguish which light station it is coming from.

Chariot: A wheeled assembly at the bottom of a Fresnel lens which is rotated around a circular track.

Clockwork Mechanism: Early lighthouses had a series of gears, pulleys and weights, which had to be wound on a recurring basis by the keepers.

Cottage Style Lighthouse: A lighthouse made up of a keeper's residence with a light on top.

Crib: A base structure filled with stone which acted as the foundation for the structure built on top.

Daymark: A unique colour pattern that identifies a specific lighthouse during the day.

Decommissioned: A lighthouse that has discontinued operating as a aid to navigation.

Diaphone: A sound signal produced by a slotted piston moved by compressed air.

Directional Light: A light which marks the direction to be followed.

Eclipse: The interval between light flashed or foghorn blasts.

Fixed Light: A light shining continuously without periods of eclipse or darkness.

Flashing Light: Alight pattern distinguished by periods of eclipse or darkness.

Focal Plane: The path of a beam of light emitted from a lighthouse. The height from the center of the beam to the sea is known as the height of the focal plane.

Fog Detector: A device used to automatically determine conditions which may reduce visibility and the need to start a sound signal.

Fog Signal: An audible device such as a bell or horn that warns seamen during period of fog when the light would be ineffective.

Fresnel Lens: An optic system composed of a convex lens and prisms which concentrate the light beam through a series of prisms. The design was produced by Augustin Fresnel in the 1800s.

Geographic Range: The longest distance the curvature of the earth allows an object of a certain height to be seen.

Isophase Light: A light in which the duration of light and darkness are equal.

Keeper: The person responsible for the maintenance and operation of the lighthouse.

Lamp and Reflector: A lamp and polished mirror used before the invention of more effective optic systems such as the Fresnel lens.

Lantern: A glass covered space at the top of the lighthouse tower, which housed the lighting equipment.

Lens: The glass optical system used to concentrate and direct the light.

Light Sector: The arc over which a light can be seen from the sea.

Lightship: A ship that served as a lighthouse.

Light Station: The lighthouse tower as well as any outbuildings such as the keeper's quarters, fog-signal building, fuel storage building and boathouse.

Nautical Mile: A unit of distance which is the average distance on the Earth's surface represented by one minute of latitude. It is equal to 1.1508 statute miles and mainly used at sea.

Nominal Range: The distance a light can be seen in good weather.

Occulting Light: A light in which the period of light is longer than the period of darkness and in which the intervals of darkness are all equal. Also known as an eclipsing light.

Order: A description of the power of the Fresnel lens ranging from one to seven from stronger to weaker.

Parabolic Reflector: A metal bowl shaped to a parabolic curve which reflects a lamp's light from it's center.

Parapet: A railed walkway which surrounds the lamp room.

Period: The total time for one cycle of the pattern of the light or sound signal.

Pharologist: A person with an interest in lighthouses.

Range Lights: Two lights which form a range provide direction to mariners for safe passage. They are described as the Front and Rear Lighthouses or the Inner and Outer. The front range light is lower than the rear, and when they align, the ship is in the proper position.

Revetment: A bank of stone laid to protect a structure against erosion from waves.

Revolving Light: A flash produced by the rotation of a Fresnel lens.

Riprap: Broken rocks or stone placed to help prevent erosion.

Sector: The portion of the sea lit by a sector light.

Skeleton Tower: Towers consisting of four or more braced feet with a beacon on top. They have little resistance to the wind and waves, and bear up well in a storm.

Solar-powered Optic: Many automated lights are run on solar powered batteries.

Spider Lamp: A brass container holding oil and solid wicks.

Tender: A ship which services lighthouses.

Ventilator: Opening' at the top of a lighthouse tower to provide heat exhaust and air flow within the tower.

Photo Credits

Alessio Damato; Tower of Hercules: **Appalachian Dreamer**; Quaco Head: **B3251**; Swift Point: **Canadian Coast Guard**; Great Duck, Machias Seal Island, Pecks Point: **Dennis Jarvis**; Belyeas Point, Caraquet Front Range, Courtenay Bay, Dalhousie Wharf, Fanjoys Point, Gagetown, Grand-Digue, Grant Beach Rear, Lower Neguac Rear Range, Oak Point Front Range, Pointe du Chene Range, Renforth, Sand Point: **Dr Wilson**; Big Shippegan, Caraquet Island: **Eaubanel**; Gannet Rock: **Fisheries and Oceans Canada**; Lower Musquash Island: **James Mann**; Grindstone Island; **Kate Wellington**; Long Point: **Marinas**; Cocagne Front Range: **Nominoe66**; Portage Island Range Rear: **Thiersch**; Pharos

All other Images by the author

The Photographer's and Explorer's Series

Unless noted, there are Print and eBook editions available for the following.

Birding Guide to Orkney
Guide to Photographing Birds

Ontario Lighthouses
Ontario's Old Mills
Ontario Waterfalls

Alabama Covered Bridges (eBook)
California Covered Bridges (eBook)
Connecticut Covered Bridges (eBook)
Georgia Covered Bridges (eBook)
Illinois Covered Bridges (eBook)
Indiana Covered Bridges
Iowa Covered Bridges (eBook)
Maine Covered Bridges (eBook)
Lighthouses of Maine
Massachusetts Covered Bridges (eBook)
Michigan Covered Bridges (eBook)
New Brunswick Covered Bridges
New England Covered Bridges
Covered Bridges of the Mid-Atlantic
Covered Bridges of the South
New Brunswick Lighthouses
New Hampshire Covered Bridges
New York Covered Bridges
Ohio's Covered Bridges
Oregon Covered Bridges
Orkney and Shetland Lighthouses (eBook)
Lighthouses of Scotland
The Covered Bridges of Kentucky (eBook)
The Covered Bridges of Kentucky and Tennessee
Covered Bridges of the North
Covered Bridges of the South
The Covered Bridges of Tennessee (eBook)
Vermont's Covered Bridges
The Covered Bridges of Virginia (eBook)
The Covered Bridges of Virginia and West Virginia
Washington Covered Bridges (eBook)
The Covered Bridges of West Virginia (eBook)

References

List of New Brunswick Lighthouses (Wikipedia)
https://en.wikipedia.org/wiki/List_of_lighthouses_in_New_Brunswick

List of Lights
https://publications.gc.ca/collections/collection_2023/mpo-dfo/Fs151-9-2023-10-eng.pdf

Lighthouse Digest
http://www.lighthousedigest.com/index.cfm

ibiblio.org
https://www.ibiblio.org/lighthouse/nb1.htm

Lighthouse Friends, New Brunswick
https://www.lighthousefriends.com/pull-state.asp?state=NB

Index

Anderson Hollow Lighthouse	10
Bayswater Lighthouse	11
Belyea's Point Lighthouse	12
Big Shippegan Lighthouse	13
Black Point Lighthouse	14
Bliss Island Lighthouse	15
Bouctouche Bar Lighthouse	16
Caisse Point Lighthouse	17
Campbellton Range Rear Lighthouse	18
Cap Lumière Lighthouse	71
Cape Enrage Lighthouse	19
Cape Jourimain Lighthouse	20
Cape Spencer Lighthouse	21
Cape Tormentine Outer Wharf Range Lighthouse	22
Cape Tormentine Outer Wharf Range Rear Lighthouse	22
Caraquet Island Lighthouse	23
Caraquet Range Front Lighthouse	24
Caraquet Range Rear Lighthouse	24
Cherry Island Lighthouse	25
Cocagne Range Front Lighthouse	26
Courtenay Bay Breakwater Lighthouse	27
Cox Point Lighthouse	28
Dalhousie Wharf Lighthouse	29
Deer Island Point Lighthouse	30
Dixon Point Range Front Lighthouse	31
Dixon Point Range Rear Lighthouse	31
East Quoddy Lighthouse	42
Fanjoys Point Lighthouse	32
Gagetown Lighthouse	33
Gannet Rock Lighthouse	34
Grand Dune Flats Range Front Lighthouse	35
Grande-Digue Lighthouse	36
Grant Beach Range Front Lighthouse	37
Grant Beach Range Rear Lighthouse	37
Great Duck Island Lighthouse	38
Green Head Lighthouse	79
Green's Point Lighthouse	39
Grindstone Island Lighthouse	40
Hampstead Wharf Lighthouse	41
Head Harbour Lighthouse	42
Hendry Farm Lighthouse	43

Inch Arran Point Range Front Lighthouse	44
Inch Arran Point Range Rear Lighthouse	44
Leonardville Lighthouse	45
Letete Passage Lighthouse	39
Lighthouse Point Lighthouse	46
Long Eddy Point Lighthouse	47
Long Point Lighthouse	48
Lower Musquash Island Lighthouse	49
Lower Neguac Wharf Range Rear Lighthouse	50
Machias Seal Island Lighthouse	51
McColgan Point Lighthouse	52
Miscou Island Lighthouse	53
Mulholland Point Lighthouse	54
Musquash Head Lighthouse	55
Oak Point Lighthouse	56
Oak Point Range Front Lighthouse	57
Partridge Island Lighthouse	58
Pea Point Light	59
Pecks Point Lighthouse	60
Pendlebury Lighthouse	76
Point Escuminac Lighthouse	61
Point Lepreau Lighthouse	62
Pointe à Brideau Range Rear Lighthouse	63
Pointe à Jérôme Range Front Lighthouse	64
Pointe du Chêne Range Front Lighthouse	65
Pointe du Chêne Range Rear Lighthouse	65
Pointe Sapin Range Rear Lighthouse	66
Portage Island Range Rear Lighthouse	67
Quaco Head Lighthouse	68
Reed's Point Light	69
Renforth Lighthouse	70
Richibucto Head Lighthouse	71
Robertson Point Lighthouse	72
Sand Point Lighthouse	73
Southwest Head Lighthouse	74
Southwest Wolf Island Lighthouse	75
St Martins Lighthouse	77
St. Andrews North Point Lighthouse	76
Swallowtail Lighthouse	78
Swift Point Lighthouse	79
The Cedars Lighthouse	80
Wilmot Bluff Lighthouse	81